marie claire

storage

acknowledgements

Karen McCartney
Many thanks to Catie Ziller for commissioning me to do this book, to Sibella Court and Hugh Stewart for producing such great images, to Anna Waddington for keeping me organised throughout, and Marylouise Brammer for such a simple, modern design execution. I would also like to thank my wonderful, patient husband David Harrison for tolerating my bouts of absenteeism.

Sibella Court
I would like to thank Dee Court for her sewing skills and general morale boosting, Chris Court for modelling and his handyman skills, and Peter Court for ladder delivery.

The publisher wishes to thank the following for their generosity in supplying props and clothing for the book: Calibre, SABA, Empire Homewears, Papaya, IKEA and Acorn Trading.

marie claire

storage

sibella court & karen mccartney
photography by hugh stewart

MURDOCH BOOKS®
Sydney • London • Vancouver • New York

contents

introduction

This is a storage book with a difference. It's not about grand-scale architectural solutions to organising space, but rather it offers a series of cleverly presented ideas that address the way we live our lives today. To a lesser or greater degree, 'stuff' is all around us. From the things we cherish and collect to the bare necessities of life, we are all surrounded by possessions which need to be grouped in order for us to maintain sanity. This book is broken down into seven chapters—lounging, dressing, working, bathing, eating, cleaning and sleeping—

and embraces a broad range of simple storage solutions. And yet the word storage doesn't quite do justice to these ideas. There is a definite cross-over with display—a sense that, if presented artfully enough, everyday objects do not need to be tucked away in cupboards but can contribute to the life and decoration of a room. By taking an inventive look at easily available products, and adapting the way in which they are used, this book provides fresh and inspirational ideas for every facet of home life.

lounging

a personal approach

There is no doubt that an ordered environment promotes a certain calm and clarity of thought, but orderliness should not be imposed at the cost of the personal and the pleasurable. Our home space is one which echoes our personalities and reflects our tastes, experiences and passions. It is therefore important that the things of life surround us, and it is how they are contained that counts. It is not about purging until only the basics are left. There is actually such a thing as disciplined clutter. It is no less rigorous than the minimalist approach, but it acknowledges that it is perfectly acceptable to collect balls of string and old buttons, as long as they have a place to live. The ideas in this book reflect that ethos. Mementos from a seaside holiday are collected in an old jam jar and tagged; a collection of these jars placed on a light-filled windowsill becomes a mini art installation that evokes fond memories of times past; a perspex box with hand-made cardboard dividers provides a place to house recipes torn from a magazine, ensuring that they have a greater chance of being used and in turn enjoyed. These ideas are about encouraging a creative approach to your living space. They tap into different ways of thinking about the everyday: about how to arrange something as commonplace as books or magazines; how to display a collection of postcards or make a virtue of necessity by keeping receipts for the tax man securely in one place. A week spent monitoring the way you really live and noting the recurring frustration points (missing car keys, the impossible-to-locate remote for the TV, finding last week's gallery opening invite) will help you define what you need. Improving your set-up—and sanity—may be as simple as fixing a hook for keys near the door, making a pouch for the remote or a pinboard for the invite.

A uniform stack of books sits neatly under a coffee table

memory jar

Take an old jam jar and fill it with holiday finds, like pebbles, feathers and shells. Include a slip of paper with the place and date.

flower press

To make a leaf or flower press, layer sheets of plywood, corrugated cardboard and white paper together and fasten with heavy webbing, available from army disposal stores.

filing box

Mix old and new: make old-fashioned cardboard dividers for a slick perspex box. Use the box to file seeds, recipes, receipts or whatever you like.

newspaper holder

Use two long pieces of strong fabric—calico, cotton drill or canvas—and sew lateral pockets wide enough to contain rolled-up newspapers or magazines. Nail or screw to the wall.

the mix

It is important that your choice of storage system complements the design spirit of the interior into which it is being placed. Visually, homes that demonstrate a consistent aesthetic approach to the functional and the decorative are generally the most pleasing. By taking an integrated approach you have a greater chance of creating a space which works on all levels. A bit of lateral thinking goes a long way when it comes to storage and display, as re-inventing and re-thinking the conventional uses of objects can add character and wit to an interior. A wooden clothes peg glued to a wall for receipts; a pot plant skate wheeled inside and piled high with art books; an old ladder used as a bookshelf; a battered suitcase filled with CDs... These are some examples of ways in which old and new can be combined to add a fresh, new dimension. Once you adopt the mind-set, you begin to see the potential of all sorts of objects. A trip to a local bric-a-brac market or hardware store takes on a new significance: weathered wooden crates can hold bottles for recycling, industrial aluminium shelving can house a magazine collection, and old glass bottles can be used as vases. Do-it-yourself is given a new twist. A contemporary cube seat is fitted out with a linen cover, complete with a side pocket for holding magazines. Modernity and DIY prove themselves perfectly compatible.

An old wooden ladder shelves a pile of books

postcard holders

A collection of postcard holders is the perfect alternative to the mantelpiece for displaying invites, cards and favourite images.

peg clip

Use a hot glue gun to stick an old-fashioned peg to a wall, or to attach a magnet on the back for use on the fridge. Use the clip for reminders, shopping lists and bills.

cube cover with pocket

Cubes made from medium-density fibreboard (MDF) make great props for casual lounging. Soften the look by customising them with homemade linen covers and adding a side pocket for holding magazines.

CD cases

Check out markets and op-shops for kids' school cases or old leather luggage. They make great stackable CD holders and are easily portable for weekends away. The dimensions of cases vary, so make sure they are ones of a suitable depth.

stacked cubes

Buy as new or make from MDF and apply a waterproof sealer. Place the cubes horizontally for low-level shelving, or go vertical and display favourite ceramics. They can even be used in multiples as a room divider.

pot plant skate

Bring the outside indoors by using a pot plant skate for piles of books and magazines. This idea is great for small-space living, or for where mobility and access are an issue.

image display

Stretch webbing from two points and use as a clothesline to attach postcards and other favourite images. Here, the paperclips are made from bamboo, but regular ones would work just as well.

wall-mounted CD stack

Readily available CD stacks work well when mounted on a wall. Choose a lightweight aluminium version and secure to the wall using a cup hook and adhesive. The stacks look good solo, in pairs or in multiples.

dressing

best foot forward

Few areas of our lives bridge our private and public selves so visibly as the clothes we wear. While it is in the home that they are cared for (or neglected) and selected, it is to the world at large that they represent our outward expression. For this reason, those unfortunate clothes combinations that result from a lack of clean alternatives just won't do. The care we give our clothes is all too evident, and storage has its part to play in looking after what we have. For most of us, our clothes are like an iceberg: the visible one-tenth is active—in constant motion from the laundry to the wardrobe to being worn—while the other nine-tenths lurk beneath the surface, rarely exposed.

For a wardrobe to be fully functioning and easy to access, you need to go through the obligatory throw out/sell/give away/recycle procedure. Abide by the rule which says that if you haven't worn an article of clothing in three years, get rid of it. It's tough but fair. After you have done the op-shop run, assess the clothes you have remaining and sort them into three categories: the stuff that can be packed away because it is for a different season; the stuff that is used infrequently (sporting equipment, or articles of sentimental value); and the everyday clothes which need to be constantly accessible. Store items in categories one and two, and concentrate on making what remains work for you.

An organdie drawstring shoe bag

storing winter clothes

Clothes with distinct seasonal use can be zipped into a calico bag (natural fibres are best, as they let the clothes breathe) and clearly labelled as to the bag's contents.

metal pegs

A row of metal bull clips can be attached to the inside of a cupboard door with hot glue or nails and used for hanging belts and other accessories.

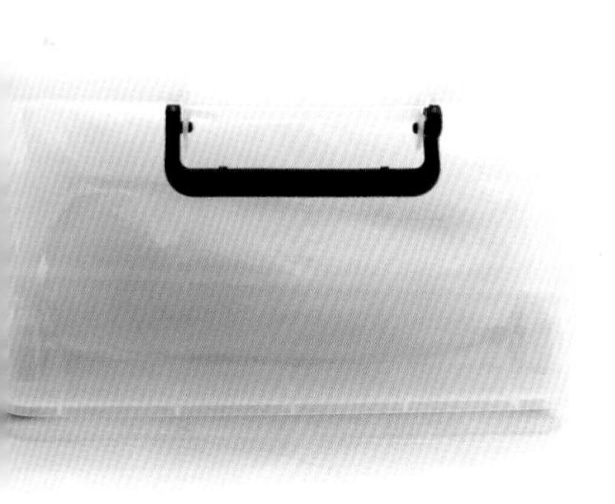

on wheels

A clear plastic container on wheels is ideal for storing winter clothes wrapped in acid-free tissue paper to help retain colour. The container can be easily slotted under the bed.

modern shoe box

Glue a clip to the front of a stackable box (size it to suit your shoe size) and clip on a printed description of the contents of the box.

P.&O.S.S

the right stuff

Effective storage is vital in facilitating a well-disciplined approach to the organisation of your wardrobe. Put simply, if you have the right amount of storage space for your clothes, you are more likely to put things away. An inadequate space means that discarded clothes more often than not end up on the floor or draped over a chair. In choosing a storage system that works, commonsense, practicality and ease of use are everything. For many people, a wardrobe is a cumbersome piece of furniture. While built-in cupboards are an obvious and appealing alternative, the trend for industrial-style fixtures and fittings has led to a range of new options. A commercial dress rail, combined with a series of plastic storage units on wheels, is a mobile, functional and inexpensive storage system. Wire baskets, hessian-covered boxes or heavy-duty cardboard or wooden crates all look great when used confidently in groups.

Of course, this kind of storage system does mean that everything is on show, so an organisational effort of another kind is required. Sort clothes into lengths, colours and types. Put each item on a single wooden hanger so that the only shirt that matches your favourite pair of trousers is not buried under four other shirts. Shoes have a habit of multiplying (sport, evening, work, leisure) and need to have their own space. Shoes are a barometer of the degree of effort you take with your appearance, and neglect shows quickly. Shoetrees may seem old-fashioned, but they work. Or you could try using soft drawstring bags that stop your shoes getting scuffed. When getting dressed, it is the small items that can be the most infuriating: the single sock, the missing strapless bra, the laddered hosiery. Weed out anything that has passed its peak, and group items of hosiery, underwear and socks in individual cloth bags, tagging them for easy reference.

Old coat-hangers make good tie racks

working

the home office

Whether you work from home or simply need to order and organise your domestic life, there is a need for a dedicated 'home office' space. Many modern apartments now come complete with a working alcove for a computer and filing systems hidden by sliding doors. In not-so-new homes we either have to content ourselves with using an area of a larger room, or dedicate a small bedroom for use as a home office. As dual-purpose spaces are common, there is a need for flexibility. A workspace by day may need to be able to transform back into a living area at night.

Visually, a workspace should echo the rest of the room. A sense of order achieved by adequate storage space will stop it appearing messy and out of control. Use old-fashioned box files in the same colour and size, and clearly label them for instant access. Mobility is another issue. Judicious use of low platforms on wheels (for computer printers), trolleys (for stationery, books and reference materials) and boxes on wheels (for filing and documents) allows for storage in corners or under tables when not in use. A light, easy-to-move screen is also useful for separating a workspace from a living space.

Take-away containers with a photocopy of their contents taped on the front

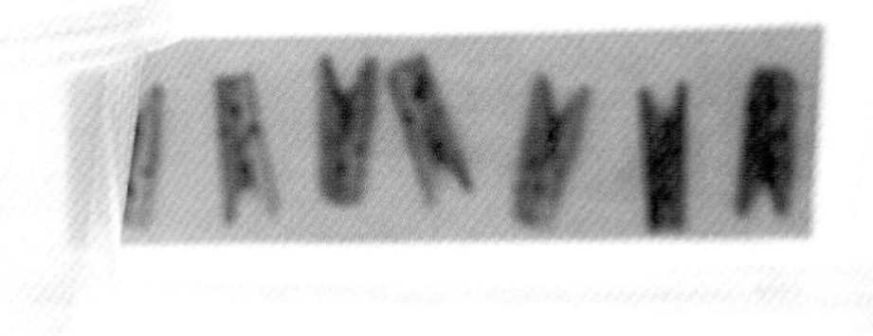
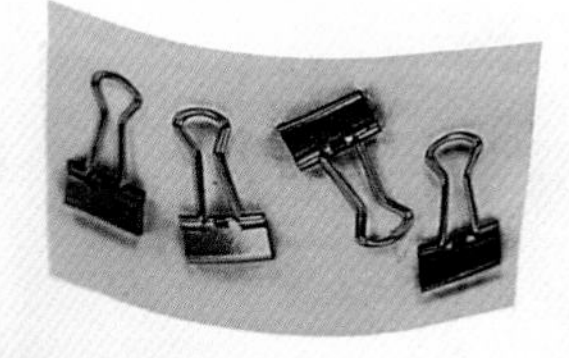

low trolley

Ideal for sliding out a computer printer from under a desk, this trolley is made from MDF sprayed with gloss enamel paint. Castors have been attached.

pencil holders

Use craft glue to cover ordinary tin cans with Chinese newspaper, then apply contact self-adhesive plastic to the outside to protect the paper.

symmetrical files

Job files can look great en masse. These cardboard-covered ones are widely available from stationery shops and come in a variety of colours.

organiser trays

A marker pen turns baking trays into effective pieces of office equipment. If the trays need to be used elsewhere, rub out the words with methylated spirits.

Job
84
Job
52

paper chase

Many of life's anxieties arise from the misplaced medical record or tax document, the unpaid phone bill and the overdue insurance policy. Several of the ideas given here introduce day-to-day options for keeping your head above the tide of paperwork. They work by providing daily, weekly and long-term solutions that are truly effortless. The paper bag hooked on the wall for holding receipts, or the old-fashioned mouse trap for pinning down bills, are immediately accessible and easy to use. You do, of course, have to revisit your bills and receipts and take action, but at least you know where they are.

Longer-term solutions to keeping track of those bits and pieces of paper come in the form of labelled cardboard boxes. Create your own filing system by whatever logic you choose to apply. Time and commitment are required—*your* time and commitment. Any system, no matter how simple, has to be set up, and you have to follow through. Popular wisdom has it that if you repeat an activity twice a day for a period of three weeks it will become habitual. Test this theory by organising your domestic or office paperwork according to one or more of the ideas given here, and see if your stress levels haven't dropped in less than a month.

A magazine rack holds numbered job files

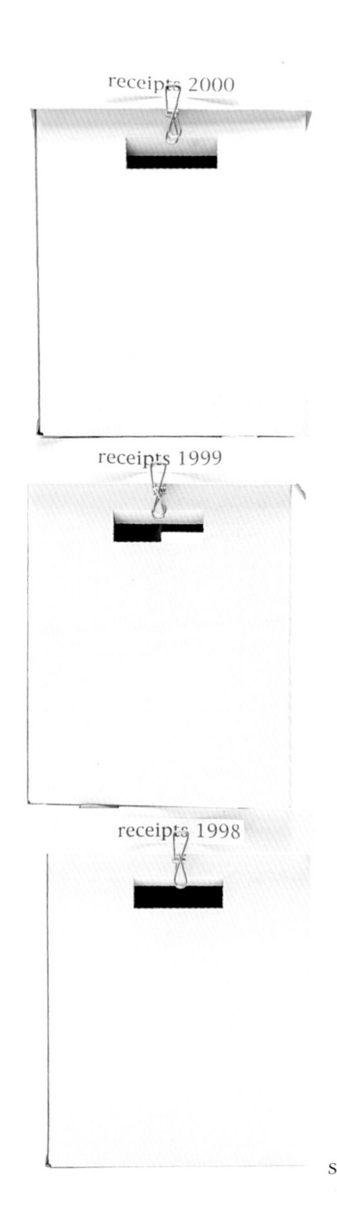

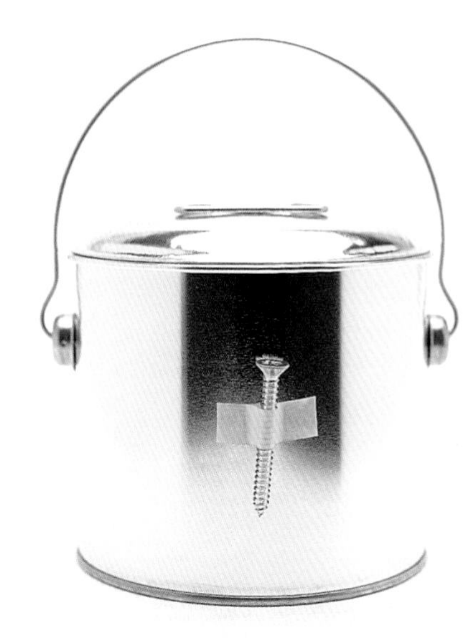

billycan hold-all

Attach a sample of the contents of a stainless steel billy to the front of the can with masking tape. A butcher's hook can be used to hang the billycan under a shelf in a handy place.

boxing clever

Collect and file receipts in utilitarian cardboard boxes that can be stacked. Bulldog clips attach labels to the lids of the boxes to describe their contents.

bag it

A suction hook from a hardware store is perfect for hooking a brown paper bag onto a fridge or a glass surface (don't attach the hook to painted surfaces). Just fix an eyelet to the bag to prevent it from tearing.

trap it

Use a hot glue gun to attach a mouse trap to a wall. Remove the hook so that it doesn't snap on your fingers, and use the trap to keep hold of small pieces of paper.

the small things

Any home office has a requisite amount of desktop paraphernalia—the calculator, the stapler, the sticky-tape holder, the post-it notes, the scissors. These are the things that need to be at hand but are never there when you want them. Equally infuriating is the difficulty of finding those small, useful things we need from time to time: the occasionally vital items that live in disparate places—at the bottom of kitchen drawers, in the woven bowls on top of the fridge. Strictly speaking they have no home, and yet you are sure you have spotted one somewhere very recently. They are the fuses, the tacks, the balls of string and the picture hooks—those items which are largely ignored until they prove to be absolutely essential. Acknowledge them and give them a home: buy stainless steel billycans and fill them with nails and screws; house bits of string and tacks in mini crates; make a tin steamer the home of a sewing kit; store clips, pegs and pins in spare plastic food containers; use baking trays as functional catch-alls for small items of office hardware. Because the small things make few space demands, they are often the hardest to tackle. But try to conquer the tiny, fiddly pieces and you'll find that those crowded kitchen drawers rendered unusable by the density of odds and sods in them will be a thing of the past.

Old metal tins are labelled by writing on broad bands of elastic

TACKS

magazine files

Standard magazine files can be purchased from any office stationer. These ones have been customised with pieces of calico. Glue a panel to the front of each box and use a pencil to describe their contents.

sewing kit

A Thai stainless steel lunchbox is ideal for converting into a multi-tiered sewing kit. Two layers should suffice, but enthusiastic sewers can stack as many as six tins on top of each other.

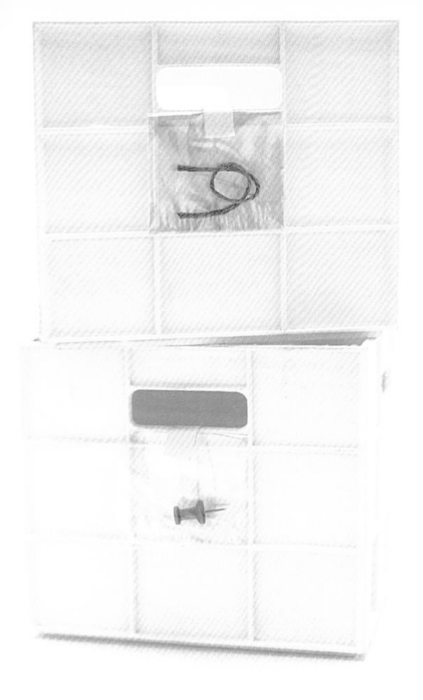

mini crates

Stackable mini crates, the desktop versions of their bigger cousins, are serviceable and durable and come in a variety of colours. Small cellophane packets taped to the front of the boxes reveal their contents.

string tidy

Turn a plain plastic box, available from a craft-supply shop, into a useful string holder. Form two eyelets by making an incision and pushing an eyelet in, then pull the string or ribbon through.

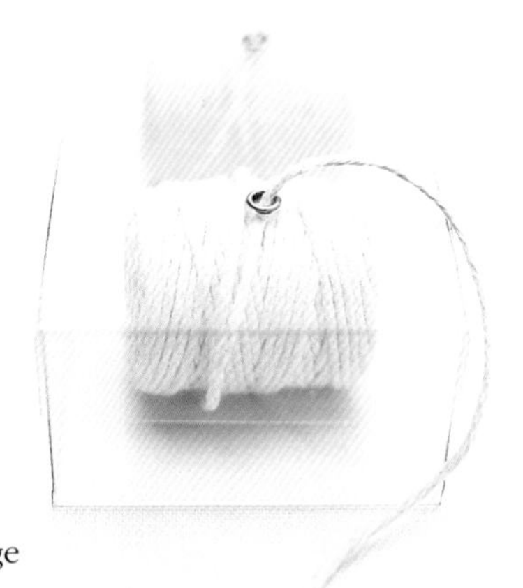

bathing

a clutter-free zone

The experience of washing means different things to different people. For some, the expectation is of hot, fast, jet showers, instant-access high-performance products and an efficient space for invigorating the body and energising the mind. For others, bathing is an experience of indulgence and recuperation, where fragrant oils and candles play their part in the relaxing, regenerating process. For these people it is an environment which combines the functional and the aesthetic. Neither approach allows for clutter. Clutter gets in the way of streamlined efficiency for one, and, as chaos is counter-culture to serenity, it conflicts with the peace of mind of the other.

The bathroom is a small space of which we often have big expectations. Not only do we wash there but we shave, apply make-up, store towels and linen, accommodate kids' bath toys and dripping swimsuits, and fill it with an endless selection of grooming, washing and medical products. And to add to its burden, it is used by every member of the household, several times a day. Clearly, it needs to be efficient and well-planned. To this end the bathroom demands a cohesive visual sense where storage items are completely in tune with the colours of the bathroom. Natural shades and materials are a safe bet—bamboo, rush and timber work well with cream and white sanitaryware.

A waterproof tray keeps essentials to hand

KIEHL'S
COCONUT

storage baskets

Finely woven rush baskets come in a range of sizes and can be used to store anything from hair accessories to economy-sized bottles.

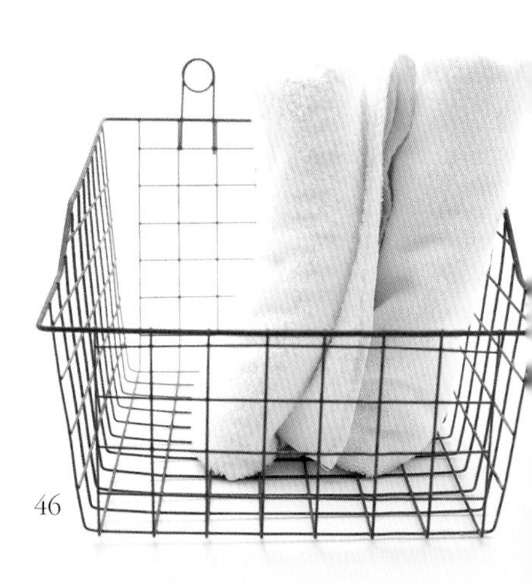

wire bicycle basket

Attached to the wall or set on a bench, this old bicycle basket is perfect for rolled-up hand towels. Check out second-hand markets for similar items.

recycled meat safe

This painted metal meat safe acts as a mini-cupboard on its own, or becomes a larger unit when stacked with a couple of other similar meat safes.

hook it on

Hang clips from a wire device more conventionally designed for curtains, and keep brushes, plugs and other bathroom items to hand by hooking them onto the clips.

a clean start

Just as it is necessary to purge your wardrobe before you can organise and streamline it, so does your bathroom need the same treatment. The bathroom is a natural breeding ground for half-used hair products that failed to live up to their promises, and old medicines and fake tanning lotions well past their use-by dates. Get rid of as much as possible. Divide the remaining products into two groups—the 'not fit to be seen' group and the 'display' group—and work out how to accommodate the former. Look at rush baskets, old metal meat safes or bamboo boxes. Whether your look is light industrial, rustic or modern, you will need several containers. Repetition works well, so don't be afraid to buy in multiples, but do make sure you have a variety of sizes to allow for small items as well as larger, economy-sized shampoos and conditioners. It is also important to try and think laterally. An old wire bicycle basket can look great filled with fresh white towels, as can railway baggage racks and bamboo ladders. Vintage jam jars make excellent containers for brushes, bamboo steamers are ideal for storing soap, and a rush basket is perfect for accommodating the all-essential toilet paper. As space is often at a premium in the bathroom, and certain products always need to be at hand, think about using the wall areas more effectively. Yachting shops can sell you wire systems which adapt well to bathroom use and allow everything from body brushes and sponges to hanging soaps to be within grabbing distance while in the shower. In the do-it-yourself spirit, a medicine cabinet or tin can be customised to give it that Red Cross feel. Hardware and homeware stores often have basic, lockable cabinets that can be sprayed a high-gloss white and decorated with a cross.

Store soap in an Asian bamboo steamer

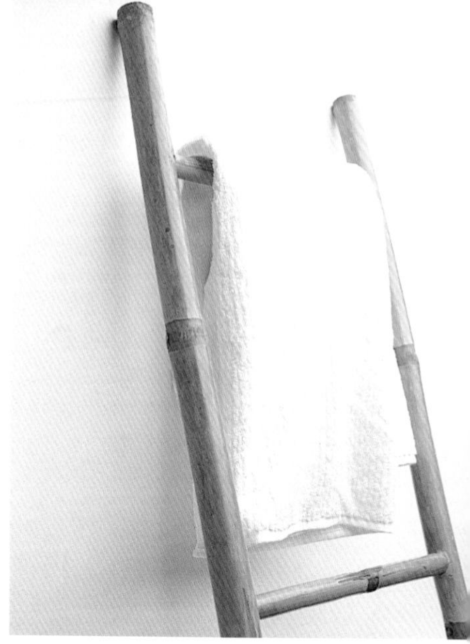

leaning ladder

Fresh, clean towels look attractive and are given a chance to air when draped over a bamboo ladder propped up against a wall.

bamboo holders

Bamboo has been cut in sections to form canisters suitable for toothbrushes and make-up brushes. This is a clever use of a natural material.

rush basket

An abundance of toilet paper is one of life's essentials. Buy a generously sized rough rush basket that is tall enough to accommodate lots of rolls.

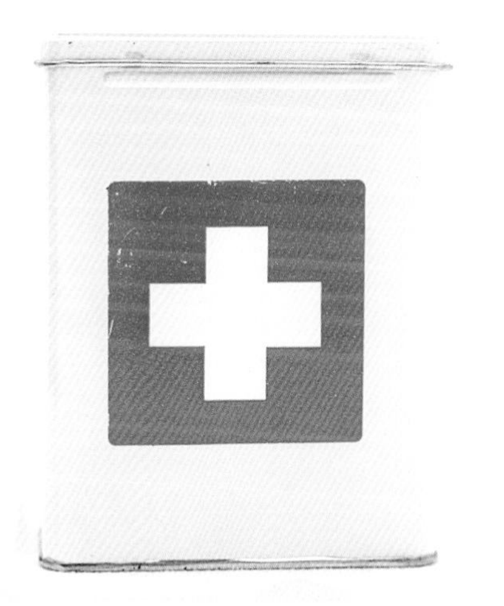

medicine tin

Keep those small medical supplies together in a custom-made tin. Spray-paint an old tin bright white and stencil on a red cross.

eating

the kitchen

The kitchen is no longer simply an area where food is prepared: it has become central to home life. These days, the formality of distinct living areas has blurred and it is often the kitchen that functions as the dining and living area. This room has to contain more stuff than any other room in the house. Not only do pots and pans inhabit this space, but a wide range of gadgets and appliances, from fridge–freezers and dishwashers to blenders and electric can-openers. Storage is essential, as it is the only way to create a functional space. The foods we eat and the way we cook has changed dramatically in the last few decades. Today's cuisine is one of speed (and, when it is good, freshness), and everything needs to be at hand. No longer does a jar of flour form the basis of our cooking. There has to be a place for kaffir lime leaves, chilli and garlic. A stir-fried meal needs a chopping board, a sharp knife, oil, salt and pepper, a wok and a wooden spoon, as well as plates, chopsticks and napkins. And all of these items need to be accessible. To make this possible, it is important to grade what you use. The everyday and attractive form one group (things you need, and things you like to look at) which can be displayed or positioned where they can be readily reached. The second group consists of those items which are used infrequently. These can be stored in cupboards (avoid keeping heavy items in low cupboards, however, as they can be inconvenient and awkward to lift). Overall, remember that the preparation of a meal won't work if the space doesn't work.

A bamboo artist's roll makes a clever cutlery holder

wicker baskets

As an alternative to drawers you might like to use open-top wicker baskets. Pile with tea towels and napkins and write their contents on luggage tags.

wire bottle holder

This unusual French bottle holder made from wire is perfect for storing wine and water for everyday drinking. Check out markets for similar finds.

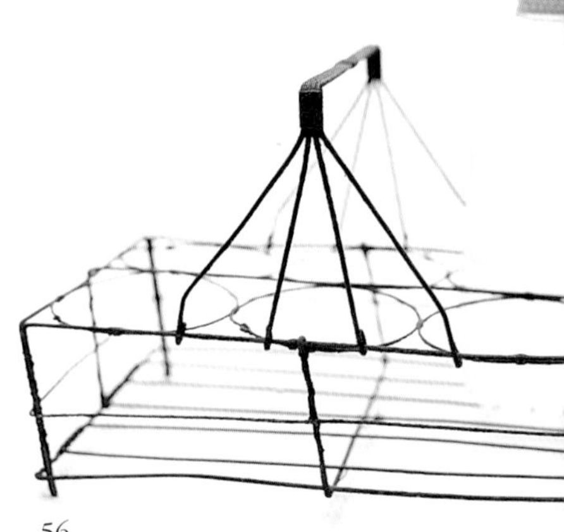

lid rack

Using the walls for storage makes space-saving sense. The lids of pots and pans slot easily into a stainless steel rail where they are close at hand.

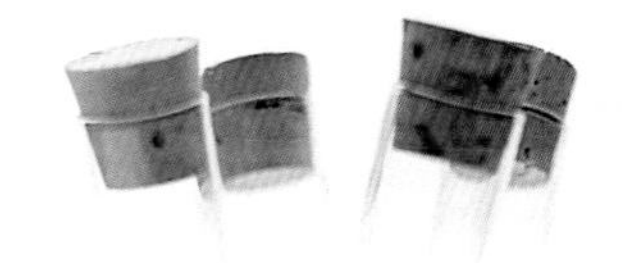

spice saver

Take the laboratory look into the kitchen. Test tubes with cork stoppers make great airtight containers for spices. Keep them together in a lab beaker or a sturdy Duralex glass.

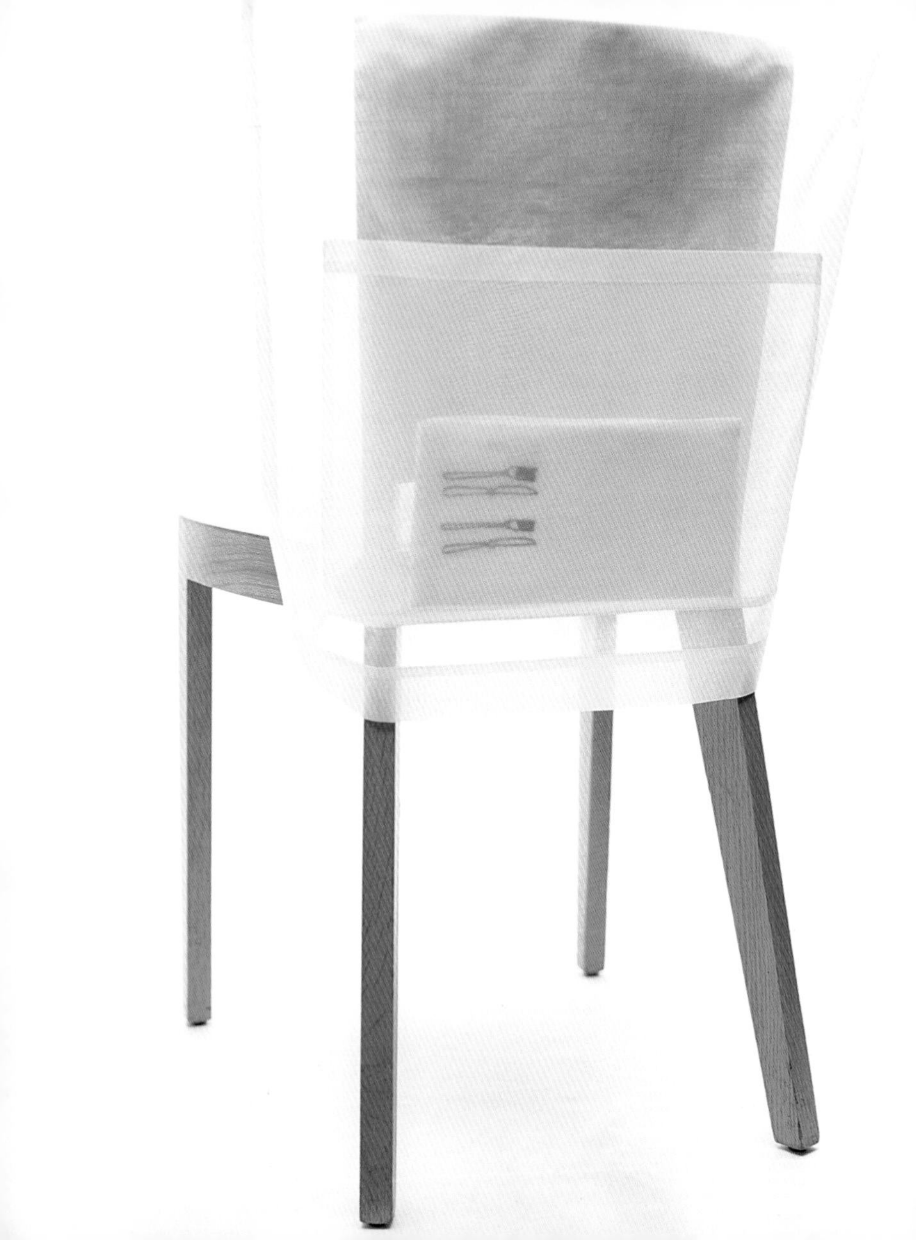

new ideas

The ideas on these pages show how to make the most of easy-to-access options and how to display the everyday. Make good use of wall and ceiling space by hanging utensils on butchers' hooks. The look can be spare or cluttered—both are effective—and you can extend the range of storage possibilities by keeping herbs in hanging wicker or wire baskets. Magnetic strips attached to a wall in rows make a strong visual statement when covered with knives and forks, and a rail for pot lids takes the angst out of hunting for that missing lid at the back of the cupboard. The kitchen also benefits from lateral uses—the laboratory test tube for spices, the slim office drawer for cutlery, the wheelie trolley for pots and pans. An inventiveness of approach is key as the move away from fully-fitted kitchens continues.

Just as cooking habits have changed, so have our eating patterns. The traditional three-course evening meal has eased up, and although it still has its place, it has given way to a more relaxed, informal approach to food, whether enjoyed shared or solo. This doesn't mean that society has descended to a collective life of TV dinners. The new mode of eating has its attendant style and rules; it is simply more flexible. A plywood tray containing a neatly folded napkin, a spoon and chopsticks and a generous bowl of noodles is no less valid than its traditional counterpart. Simple storage solutions reflect this move. A wire bottle carrier for ready-to-drink wine or water, a bamboo steamer filled with sticky Asian condiments or a basket full of easy-to-grab napkins reflect a new portability that integrates storage into the daily eating ritual.

An organdie slip cover with cutlery and napkin in the pocket

alternative tray

A Chinese steamer makes a useful and decorative tray for sticky condiments. Any drips can soak into the absorbent bamboo base.

hang it all

A rack hung with butchers' hooks is perfect for kitchen utensils and for baskets holding chillies and garlic. The rack can be as long as the kitchen space permits.

out of the office

Office storage works equally well in the kitchen. Here, a cutlery tray has been inserted into a thin file drawer and labelled accordingly.

glass jars

These surgical jars come in a wide range of sizes and look good filled and displayed. They are economical to buy and have the added benefit of being completely airtight.

strip storage

A magnetic strip traditionally used solely for sharp knives can also be used for all sorts of stainless steel cutlery. Buy multiple strips and use them for knives, forks and spoons.

stackable jars

These durable, square glass jars are easy to stack. Cut out the label from the original food packet and you will always be able to tell what is inside.

vintage bowl

When is a fruit bowl not a fruit bowl? When it's a colander. Multi-purpose kitchen buys make sense, especially when serviceable items are as beautiful as this old colander.

folded napkin

By folding and pressing a napkin into a pocket it becomes a natural hold-all for cutlery and chopsticks. It works well as a display idea for a dinner party.

cleaning

domestic duties

Cleaning is one of life's necessities. By keeping it streamlined and functional you can also make it quick. For this to be possible, the essential equipment must be at hand, ready to facilitate a smooth-running domestic life. A few items will stand up to display but, realistically, when it comes to cleaning products, most are best kept hidden. If hiding them is not possible, try disguising cleaning fluids by carefully transferring them into old-fashioned bottles (always keep out of reach of children, however), or enclose ugly packets in shiny tin containers. By hooking mops and brooms in cupboards they are out of sight and take up no floor space. This storage idea can be extended to include all sorts of appliances: plastic bags, cleaning cloths in net bags, buckets. This method of storage also has the practical advantage of ensuring that cloths and mops dry quickly, since the air is able to circulate around them.

The natural bias in cleaning equipment is towards wood and aluminium. This creates an achievable style statement, from the cheapest of solutions, like a large tin can stripped of its label and used as a container, to an industrial-style garbage bin on wheels. With bins, consider recycling solutions. Buy in pairs and use one for bottles and paper, or opt for stackable, space-efficient crates. Re-invent a bait basket as a container for clothes pegs, or transform a woollen sock into a hold-all for a shoe polishing kit. You can also convert certain objects into storage items in their own right. A basic aluminium mop bucket takes on a new life with an easily made calico pocket system, making it useful for gardening equipment, cleaning implements or tools. Every household needs a system for laundry, and using wall space as opposed to floor space is a clever solution. A series of drawstring laundry bags allows for colours to be separated.

A custom-made calico hold-all has been fitted to a standard aluminium mop bucket

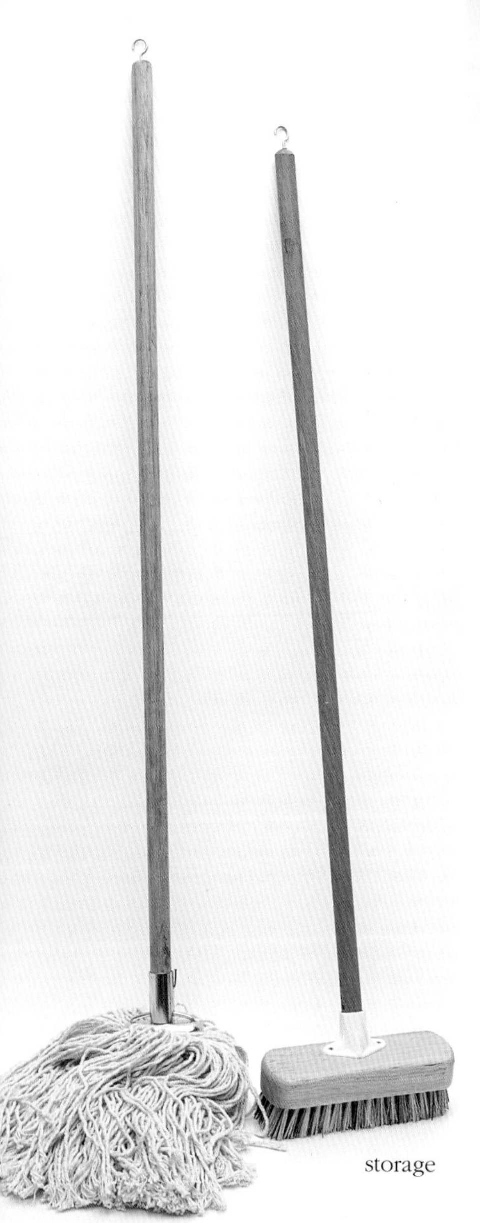

glass and steel

A clinical approach to storing cleaning products goes with the territory. Stay sharp with stainless steel canisters and old-fashioned bottles that say it how it is.

brush and mop

Get brushes and mops out of sight by attaching cup hooks to the ends of the handles and hanging them up in a cupboard or against a laundry wall.

sock it

Attach a loop of webbing to a thick woollen sock and fill the sock with shoe polish, cloths and brushes. Hook to the inside of a cupboard for easy access.

clothes pegs

An old wicker bait basket is ideal for tying to the clothes line and filling with pegs. The open weave ensures that rainwater doesn't collect inside it.

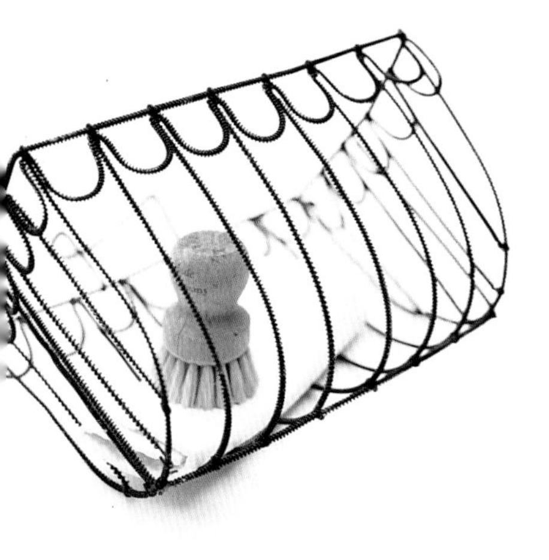

wire frame

Designed specifically to hook onto the side of a bath, this decorative wire frame is a useful addition to a laundry sink. It keeps a scrubbing brush and washing cloth to hand.

laundry bags

Buy or make three simple drawstring bags and hook them onto a wall in the laundry. Tag each one to identify the correct type of wash: whites, coloured or hand wash.

tin container

A tin can is a good and cheap way to create instant storage. Use solo to keep cleaning materials together, or en masse in a workshop for brushes or fiddly nails and screws.

wheelie bin

A large aluminium bin on castors is useful not only in the kitchen but in the home office, where lots of paper may need to be recycled. Or you could fill it with ice and wine for parties…

sleeping

sanctuary

The bedroom is our most personal space, the place where we are most ourselves. This also makes it a natural environment for gathering clutter. At the end of the day we often don't have the energy to put our clothes away, to remove the crockery from the morning's tea and toast, or to clear out the weekend papers. This means that instead of being a sanctuary in which to re-energise, it becomes a disorganised space that increases, rather than eases, our stress levels. On average we spend an astounding one-third of our lives in bed. As the bedroom becomes an increasingly multi-functional space, that amount of time increases. The bed no longer becomes just a place for sleeping. In the bedroom we can listen to music, watch television, read, talk on the telephone, eat and even work. With all these possibilities, it becomes difficult to maintain the serene, pared-down environment necessary in a bedroom.

Storage plays its part in simplifying things. Canvas pouches straddling the width of the bed on a band of cloth placed between mattress and base are ideal for books. Low, mobile storage units can hold papers and a laptop computer which slide out from under the bed, and leather boxes storing extra blankets can double as a bedside table. It is a matter of considering what you need and planning a place for it.

A bed is subject to seasonal changes, so extra storage will need to be found for bed coverings that are not in use. Roll up winter quilts in wicker baskets, or stack linen in boxes which fit under the bed. If they are visible, make sure the boxes are attractive. It is not only large items that need to be stored: the bedroom falls prey to the tyranny of small things. Bedside tables become littered with safety pins, laundry dockets and loose change. Get a series of containers, fill them up and periodically give accumulated coins to charity.

A calico bed-pocket for magazines and books hangs over the side of a bed

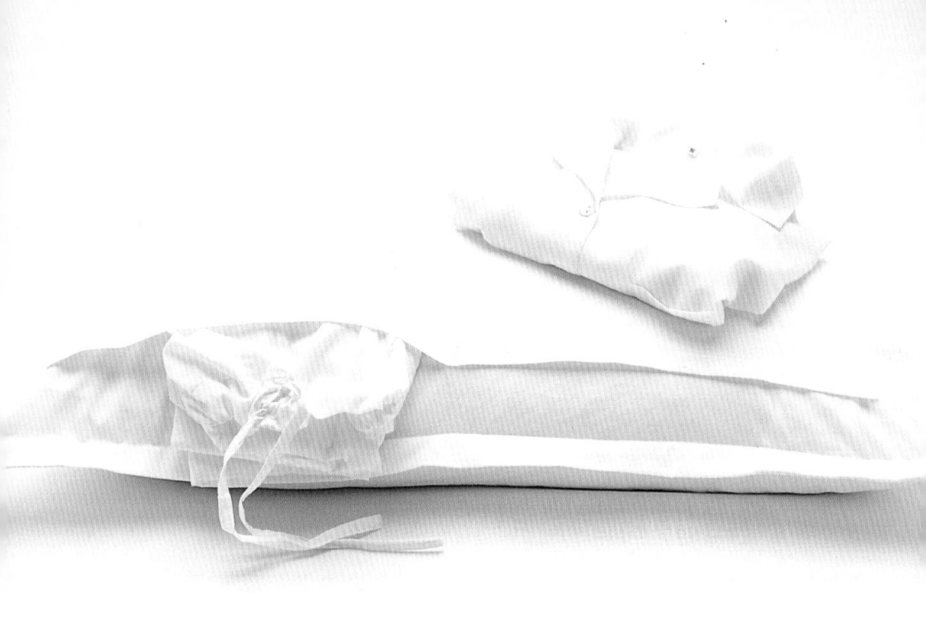

a place for PJs

A rectangular piece of cotton that matches the fabric of the pillowcase has been stitched on top of the pillow-case to make a pouch for pyjamas.

double function

A beautifully crafted object like this leather box acts as a bedside table. At the same time, it allows papers or magazines to be kept safely inside.

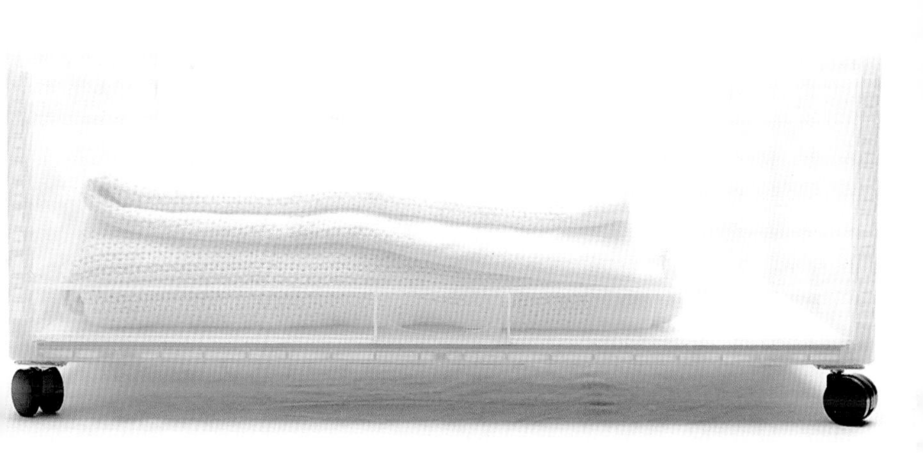

mobile box

Castors have been screwed into a large plastic box to create a trolley which can be rolled out from under the bed whenever needed.

winter quilts

A large bamboo basket is perfect for displaying and storing rolled-up winter quilts, layered blankets and spare sets of bed linen. The open weave of the basket allows stored items to be aired.

TOYS

toy storage

Some of the most difficult items to manage in terms of storage are children's toys. Nothing quite prepares you for the sea of plastic, the alarming size of the toys and the multitude of tiny pieces that make up many games. It is a daunting task, but try to sort out, throw out or give away toys which are no longer used. Kids like to have things easily accessible and within reach, so simple solutions please them. Long, wide shelves are good because boxes and books can be stacked both on them and under them. In small spaces, think vertical. Traditional bunkbeds are these days being remodelled to include storage areas at the ends and even underneath the bed. Or you could simply elevate a bed to form a platform and use the space underneath for built-in cupboards and open shelving. Any system which encourages kids to tidy up after themselves is a virtue. Large drawstring bags are great for containing dressing-up clothes; plastic tool boxes (available from hardware shops) are ideal for the Lego collection; jam jars are good for storing coloured pencils and pens; and coloured cardboard boxes are suitable for puzzles and games. Turn calico book bags into toy bags that can be hooked up beside the bed for day-and-night access to those vital toys.

A book bag has been turned inside-out and customised with felt lettering to make a toy bag

Index

This edition published in 2000 by Merehurst Limited, Ferry House, 51–57 Lacy Road, Putney, London SW15 1PR.

Published by Murdoch Books®, GPO Box 1203, Sydney, NSW Australia 1045.

Author: Karen McCartney
Stylist: Sibella Court
Photographer: Hugh Stewart
Concept & Design: Marylouise Brammer
Project Manager: Anna Waddington
Editor: Susan Gray
Model: Chris Court

CEO & Publisher: Anne Wilson
Associate Publisher: Catie Ziller
General Manager: Mark Smith
Production Manager: Liz Fitzgerald
International Sales Director: Kevin Lagden
Sales & Marketing Manager: Kathryn Harvey

A catalogue record for this book is available from the British Library.
ISBN 1 85391 911 X.

Printed by Toppan Printing Hong Kong Co. Ltd. PRINTED IN CHINA. First printed 2000. Distributed in the UK by Macmillan, Houndmills, Basingstoke, Hampshire RG21 6XS. Telephone (0) 1256 329242